Submerge In Beauty

Veronia Wilson

Dear Readers,

Submerge in Beauty, poems connecting human identity in different aspect of living.
With human identities there is always a hint of natures that whiffs through and through. We all connected to life in all forms that a hint of delicacy and serenity is always forthcoming as we stand to look at animal in nature.
Everything connect as they all makes our lives beautiful just the way it is.
Let love create unity in us always.
-Veronia Wilson

Getting to the finishing

line of joy is happiness.

-   Veronia Wilson

Table of Contents

6. Senorita

13.In the stream of life

28.Being a part of nature

40.Human identity

50.Animal

65.Delicacy

74.Serenity

92.The depth of life

107.About the author

SEÑORITA

8. Goodbye

10. Lady Magenta walk

12. An evening by Lady Magana

Goodbye

The ribbon slip through her
fingers sliding up and into
the air flowing into the evening
sunset.
Lost and forgotten.

As Sheba close her eyes.
Tears flowing down her cheeks.
As she say goodbye to a close
chapter of love lay to rest.

She put her bag on her shoulder
While placing a single red rose
on the grave of a man no more.

A thunder flash, as cold outburst
of showers cascade down on her
mournful outfit.

As she lift her face to the pelting
rain.
She mentally say a prayer of

thank while bolting to the
waiting car of friends.

......love at time strikes only
once or not at all.
It's better to be love than
never.
Goodbye my love...she whispers.

Lady Magenta Walk

Walking through the meadow
She stop as she plucked a single
tulip.
Growing between some grass.

She raise her hand
Over her eyes to block out the
sunlight.
As she look at the herd of horses.

She continued to walk passing
a few horses grazing while feeding
their youngs.

She drew in a small breathe
as she smell the scent of the tulips.
There was a small spring flowing by.

She knelt down, while using her
palms to scoop up some refreshing
water.

Bringing her palms to her lips

She swallow the soothing liquid.

She then sit by the spring enjoying
the rustling sound of water.
While she close her eyes for a bit.

She sit like that for a time
Then she open her eyes
To look at the water flowing overs
stones and little fishes swimming by.

She heard the clapping sounds
of feets.
As some of the horses draw near.
To get a drink by the spring,

She dust off her pants
getting up.
To make the trip back.

Passing the herds of horses as
she go.
She pick a bunch of tulips of
multi colors.
For a vase well deserved.

An Evening by Lady Magana

Lady Magana sit in her dressing
room.
When she stand, she look into her
carved Venetian mirror.
While brushing her jet black hair,
She brush for awhile
As she looked at the brush sliding
through her black hair.
She place the brush onto her vanity chair.
She then lay on her Victorian chaise lounge.
To take a well deserved rest.
She look at the beautiful draperies that
highlight her windows.
She then graceful walk to her window
Where she pause as she slides her hands
on the draperies before pushing it aside.
To look at the busy street out side.

IN THE STREAM OF LIFE

15. The days goes...while life continues

16. The night comes…while life continues

17. The break of day

18 In the stream of life

21. Slowdown...what if

24. Nothing is as it appears

25. The truth of life

26. The nature of life is spirited

The day goes...while life continues

The crickets still chirping in the
morning light.
While the roosters crows for
breakfast.

The moon still takes her stroll
across the sky.
While the sun wait patiently to
ride to a bright day.

The dog yawn and stretch
While looking at me with lazy
eyes.

The breezes blow cool air to
great the morning hue.
While across the horizon was
looking exquisite with beautiful
array of trees.

The night comes….while life continues

I still hear the shout from the children.
While they play in the evening sunset.

The hush of the day gather around and
Seattle like a warm blanket.
While the chicken are busy gathering
their youngs to be sheltered under a
tree.

You can smell the sweet aroma of
dinner cooking tingling the evening
air.
While neighbors closes windows and
doors to settle in, to a evening of
togetherness.

The break of day

I think I shall never see
The break of a day
With sunshine so beautiful and
breathtaking.
A day where the sun warm my
bones while my skin tingle with
delight.

A day where I lay lazily under a
tree.
While sunlight glisten and dance
between the leaves.
While the sun ignites the earth and
lift the crust in patterns of boxes of
array that cover its surface.

A day when fowls scattered dirt
to form a nest to pick and play
as the sun warm their bodies.

In the stream of life

In the stream of life.
It's like flowing through chapters
and chapters of living.

Spending a day or a full week
Every single seconds into a man,
or a woman life.
Sitting with a man or a woman as
they talk about their most darkest of
secrets.
In their bedrooms, bathroom, closets.
In their most precious moments of their lives.
Yes seeing the life they live, that's hidden
away from the public eyes.
Amazing to see ordinary life of living.

Going into the water
Spending time with aquatic life
Seeing their up and around in full.
Moving with a school of fish, hanging
out with the Dolphins.
Living with the Sharks as they tear
dolphins, fishes and many more from

limb to limb.
What uprise to rest on a soul.
Who follow only one foot steps; his.

Going into the forest spending days
on an individual lives of different
vicious animals.
It will be a little put out to find yourself
a buffalo being chased by a lion.
While they eat and then run for
their lives.
Stumbling over, while getting up and
running for your life.
Being in a stamped, frightened, being
caught as a lion clasp his
mouth around your neck
Feeling life slipping away slowly
while your skin is tearing viciously
by an hungry or many hungry lions.

You the lion body flustered with
fun and excitement, heart racing
while it is still beating with strained.
The waiting has now come to a close,
prool no more, aggressively you bite
into the warm flesh of the buffalo,
hard cold teeth tearing, enjoying

dinner.
Th catch of the day.

Slow down……what if

We as humans sometimes
simple things of this world we
are not happy with.
We do not realizes that things
are what they are.

The basic of life sometime never
please our lives.
We wish nature was different.
We hate what nature gives us.
A harmonize world.

We think too much rain, sun,
snow.
Or
Too little rain, sun, and snow.
But could we stop and look at
wha if…

The rain slow down
Or speed up.
Too much rain is flood and less
rain is drought.

What if
We have too much sunshine.
will crate drought and animals,
plants and humans will have
sun stroke and some will perish
if not all.

Or less sunshine.
Plants, animal, and humans will
takes longer to grow, famine,
skin rash and extreme Poverty and
death.

What if
Countries that have snow get less
snow.
No problem, cheers we are happy.

But what if……
Countries that have snow gets too
much snow.
Oh, no untold mayhem.

We need to enjoy this world with our
in tack seasons.
While we pray that the rain, the sun,

the snow and many more changes
throughout the years never get
speed up like a tsunami
Or
slow down like an hurricane.
Who would know when the eye of the
Storm would actually past.

Slow down……… What if
they speed up.

Nothing is as it appears

The deep blue sea
That shimmers in the sun.
Up on contact it's crystal clear.

The blue sky
That seem near yet far.
As long as man journey up
into the sky.
Not will he sees a blue sky;
optical illusions.
But a sky of unfathomable
depth.
Fills with many of wonders.

The breezes that blows.
Everyone of us feels the breezes
as it blows.
It rustle the leaves as it passes
through the trees.
It scattered dust, lift things and
swirls them into the air.
Yet man have never seen nor touch
the breezes.

The truth of life

This world that we grow up in.
Everything Is changing in this
world.
Mankind is evolving.
Everyday of his natural life.
His ideas, his philosophy is evolving.

Mankind is creating a new, everyday.
So whatever you might leave at a
certain spot in the past
You may never comes back and
find it their.
Someone will replace it.

Just like any great ideas.
Life is a constant changing event.
The rich can get poor.
The poor can get rich.

There is only one law in the universe
that never changes.
That all things change and that all
things are impermanent; not lasting.

The nature of life is spirited

The nature of life is spirited
Man look at life as a baby
looking at a toy.
Happy moments.
Sad moments.
Man hardly ever think about anything
beyond what he is now living.

Man hardly stop to think about.
Why the sun shines.
Why the birds sing.
Why the sea wash ashore,
unmove by simple fetter.
Why the sea inhabitants never
comes to shores.

Why today alway arrives
and there's always a tomorrow.
This world a world without an end.

Mankind just eat, drink and sleep.
Hardly if ever think about this big
wide world.
That we live into.
Mankind only inhabited earth out
of too many planets and galaxies.

The nature of life, spirited as usually.
Undefine for who hardly ever look.
Define for who sees with an open
eyes.

The nature of life is spirited.
Man look at life as a baby
looking at a toy.
Happy moments.
Sad moments.
Man hardly ever think about
nothing beyond what he is now
living.

BEING A PART OF NATURE

30. The wind

31. The Meadow

32. The rain fall

34. The sun

35. Leaves

37. Flowers

38. The weather

The Wind

Blowing throw the forest.
The wind sings as she
dances throw the leaves.

The trees swings happily,
as leaves fall softly
on the ground.

It's a joyous sound
To hear the melody
created by nature.

So, as the wind caresses
the checks of her loyal servants.
They rejoice triumphantly
to be able to create melody of
sounds.

The Meadow

Running through the meadows
laughters of sound.
Children with butterflies nets
And soft little hands.

You can hear such
soft voices of laughters
As they giggles with joy.

Each with their presents
Of beautiful butterflies.
To be cherish and admires
days to come.

The Rain Fall

Standing by the door
watching the rain.
It's like soft spike flowing
down.

Shee goes the rain.
with bouncing droplets
making muddy streaks
flowing by.

As my ears pick up the
waves of the sounds
cascading.
I listen with wonderful
delight.

As the rain wet the leaves
It makes a soft splash
As it glides to the ground.

Soft droplets
That's cold to the touch.
Caressing the ground

The rain fall.

The Sun

The sun has put its
self out in its glittering
of shine.

Dark clouds surround the
sun in its peak of
perfection.

Nimbostratus has hid
the sun.

In an twinkle of an eye
The sun once again shines
in perfection.

The dark clouds scattered
once more as the sun slides
down the horizon.

Between blue sky and
cumulonimbus clouds
the sun shines luminous.

Leaves

The beautiful leaves in the
autumn breezes.
Such opulent bouquet of red,
orange, and gold.
What dazzling and sensation.
To see leaves displaying such
yellow and Crimson decors.
Nature producing leaves in a
flowering display.

The beautiful leaves that's spring
creates.
It's the time of the year for
blooming.
And breathtaking as usually with
the evergreen.
Plus the mosaic of colors of
different leaves.

Yellow the creation of summer
leaves,
Bright and beautiful.
After that beautiful decor of

yellow.
New sprout of rich, green leaves.
The beauty of newly grown buds.

Leaves running with a shade of
winter snow.
Frosts that leave leaves sparkles.
Beyond the cold is leaves with
beautiful shade of divine colors
that the eyes can see.

The diversity and uniqueness
of beautiful colors leaves.
The changing of nature.

Flowers

Such beautiful decors of flowers
Flowers with boys name.
Kunal the lotus.
Yellow Saffron.
Narcissus my daffodil.
My rose bud Jarred.

Flowers with girls name.
Dew of the sea my Rosemary.
Dahlia the beauty.
Zinnias such beauty and adoration.
Camellias bestow with such creamy
fragrance.

Flowers; carnation florists choice.
Orchid, Peony, Sunflowers, Tansy,
Tulip, Violets, Marigold, Forget Me
Not, Bird of Paradise, Baby breathe.
Flowers soft like Buttercup.
Adores like Peach Blossom
and fragrance like Lavender.

The Weather

The weather is dangerously
pique by the torrential rain
fall.

The violent windstorm twist
the smiling sun in a downward
frown.

The dust cries angrily in surprise
as it was pick up from the ground
and hurl in the air by a swirling
motion.

The sea was astonished to
wake up wearing dark brown
dye on her beautiful blue curls.

The clouds cry heavily throughout
the week bringing forth large
quantities of raindrops.

The gentle breezes smile in
amazement as he blow gentle

throw the trees.

The water flow throw the rocks
Springing forth cool spring
water.

The river stream past many
creeks on its way to town.

HUMAN IDENTITY

42. A day at the beach

44. My purple sweater

46. Love the healing of nature

47. Enchantment

49. To fall in love

A day at the beach

Has I walk on the sand
little crabs shuffles by.
I press my feet into the sand
As wave of water splashes to
shore.

Little boys and girls are
laughing.
As they build sand castles.
While moms and dads lay on
towels tanning away.

I continue to walk
Passing teenage boys and girls
playing volleyball with enthusiasm.

I pass the lifeguard surfing the
at the humongous crowd of
happy swimmers.

Ouch, I said as a ball comes hurling
into my chest.

Sorry mom they shouted as I kick
the ball to a group of boys.

You could hear splashes and shouts
of happy laughters.
I see surfers on boards
While a few were lying
lazily in the sun.

As I gather my thoughts surrounding
by whirlpool of happiness
I dive into the sea to enjoy.
A day at the beach.

My Purple Sweater

Once I had a purple sweater.

Everyday I wore that purple sweater.

Even when I am with friends I wore
that purple sweater.

I came home early one day and
I could not find my purple sweater.

I turn the house upside down looking
for that purple sweater.

Only later I discovered that my aunt
has come and borrowed my purple
sweater.

Never again will I feel the comfort of
that purple sweater.

I shed a few tears thinking about
that purple sweater.

How I miss and wish I had my purple sweater.

Once I had a purple sweater.

Love the healing of nature

Love is usual the healing of
nature.
And the beauty of the sunsets.
While the birds fly to their nests.
And lovers walk with joyous steps.

Love as usual romance in the air.
Wisk of twilight, lovers enjoyed
candle light.
As they whispers secrets of love
Melody only they can hear.

Love as usual the laughters of
children.
So young, so happy, so innocent
and gay.
Children making small steps of
growing and enjoying life.

With love we build on hope and
adventure.

Enchantment

Enchantment, bliss, sweet romance.
Gosh ain't we all carving hungrily
for Prince Charming.

Someone to swarm our being with
love.
Sweet, sweet togetherness.
A fairy tale love that goes on
and on.

Someone to kiss us breathtakingly
Someone to take our breath away.
Someone to shower us my God with
showers of breathtaking kiss.

Someone to open heaven's gate
A sharer, a understander, a admirer,
a cultivator of love.
Someone to understand life.

Someone to enchanted our life.
An enchanter
An enchantment of eternal love

always.

To fall in love

To fall in love
Is to be inspired
With feelings that cannot be
identified by simple words.

To fall in love
Is to feel in depth.
In your being this touch of
something special.

To fall in love
Is to realize a new
That every moment in life
is precious.

To fall love
Is to know that love
is something awaken in your mind.
Opening up like a ray of hope.

ANIMAL

52. The Majestic Flyer

53. Submerge in beauty

56. The crocodile

58. Bluebird

60. The Dragon

61. The Yak curiosity

62. Wendy Kewe Boo

The Majestic Flyer

Looking up into the sky.
At the majestic flyer soaring past.
What impressive beauty.
Bestowed with such fine feathers.
Gliding, a glimpse of grace and
eloquence.

As I pause with waiting breathe
The majestic flyer perched with
dignity and magnificence.
Showing off rainbow of glowing
colors.

Off again soaring upward
To grace the sky
On to new adventure
The majestic flyer.

Submerge In Beauty

The soft flower petal blowing in
the wind.
Dance as the wind caresses it,
flowing in the air.
It swirled in the autumn breeze
before it lay gentle into the lake.

The beautiful swan swimming
gracefully in the lake.
She bowed her long graceful
neck.
Looking down at her reflection
of pure magnificent.

The herring startled by the swan
reflection.
Dive down into the water for a
sudden escape.

There was a loud uproar by children
 who we're admiring the swan as
she lift her long neck and make a
song of joy.

The pigeons who were busy eating
some left over corns startled by the
sudden uproars of the children,
flutters off in dismay.

A stray cat who was watching the
pigeons from a far.
Emerge with a flight of annoyance
as the flock take their leave.

A man who was passing busy on
his phone, step on the cat tail.
The cat leap up in surprise in the
air knocking over a little girl who
was busy eating an ice cream cone.

The little girl was taken up by a lady
who saw what had happen and take
her to a vendor and bought her an
ice cream.

The lady then make a leave of
absent to go and collect the group
of children by the lake who were
observing the graceful swan.

The children make another uproar
of gratitude at the swan as she
cuddle her babies in comfort.
The children bid their goodbye
and farewell.

The Crocodile

Lying lazily in the sun.
He yawns as he watches
the shadow of the sun take
a leave of absence behind some
clouds.

He pushes up his body
As he shuffle off to take
comfort between some trees.

He snores for some time
beneath the trees as wind
blow over his body.

He wake with a startled.
Fly scattered as he open
his eyes to view the distance
to shuffle off.
To the calm of the muddy lake.

As he look at the muddy stream
of still water.
He make a run and slide into

the sluggish water
Diving under.

He stayed under for a while
before rising up his head
once more to view his surrounding
before going under once again to
close the chapter of a day gone
and forgotten.

Bluebird

Bluebird, bluebird in and out
the window.
There was once this beautiful
bluebird in the place garden.

Everyday the beautiful princess
would sit and listen to the bluebird
sings while she kit her beautiful
fabric.

The little bluebird has this beautiful
voice that you could hear it singing
throughout the place garden.

One day the princess was sitting
by the window
But she could not hear the bluebird
sings.

Months as come and past and she
did not her the bluebird.

The princess woke early one

morning to hear her bluebird singing
the most loveliest of song she had
ever heard.

Rushing off to look out her window
it was the bluebird her mate and three
lovely baby birds.

The bluebird had when away mate
and return with her family.
It was the most breathtaking of sight
that ever behold the princess eyes.
She dance and sing with joy
Her bluebird had return.

The Dragon

Flying in the mid-night breezes.
Resting for a minute or two.
As they carry out their duty
Protecting the innocent.

The dragon
The ensure of good luck.
Wealth and prosperity
Guardian of their own treasures.
Guardian of their own land.

The dragon
Legendary animals
Breather of fire
A beneficent symbol of fertility
Associated with water and the
heaven.

The Yak Curiosity

The yak is a domesticated wild
ox.

Both sex of the yak carried
horns.

Both sex have long shaggy
hair.

They have long horse like
tails.

They are also used for racing
and plowing fields.

Yaks are used for their milk,
meat, and hide.

Yaks do not eats grains only
grass and herbs.

Wendy Kiwe Boo

That's Wendy walking around the
yard.
Showing her teeth as she go.
I say, this dog is a laughter this
one.

She sport a game face that light
up like a Christmas tree.
Whenever you are near her.

I called her Wendy but my son
called her Wendy Kiwe Boo.
The charm of a dog which I had
never seen before.

It's more than just a smiling face.
She talks in only a language at
time I wish I know.

How at times I know she would
wow me with tales and horror of
stories bestown to me yet.

The depth and passion which
Wendy communicate with
Is a surprise twist.

I remember once when trouble
brew, I think my oldest child was
late from school and I was a
bit trouble.

As I stand there with my washing
brush in my hand.
Wendy run up to me as she looketh
at me.

She put words to meaning as I
understand not her complain,
but she did communicate for awhile.

Still then I remember Wendy was
on the verge of delivering some pups.
I was resting underneath a star apple
tree.

And she comes to me trouble as she
speak and speak.
I then rub her down for awhile
She was their relax for sometime

Before the day end.

Wendy produce that day some healthy
pups.
Such beauty to be marvel about.
But one thing I know for sure Wendy
is hardly seen without a smile on her
face and few good words to
communicate with.
That's Wendy Kiwe Boo.

DELICACY

67. The Chocolate cake

69. Strawberry

70. Food

72. My vegan Dishes

The Chocolate Cake

My mouth run water
As I look at the chocolate cake.
With exquisite oft texture of
chocolate swirls lacing the edge.
How lovely the icing look sitting
on the cake.

My eyes bulge as my taste buds
kick up speed.
As I try to count the many juicey
red cherries on top.

Between the cherries are lace work
of art.
Beautiful snowflake of soft white
flowers.
Adoring the intricacy of chocolate
cake.

My heart started to throb in distress.
As my palms get sweaty and sweaty.
I continues to rub my palms on my
skirt as I decided which side to cut

the chocolate cake.

I stamp my foot in distress
As I tumble over and over in my
mind the delicacy of that
mesmerizing chocolate cake.

I started to feel this gentle shake
as I force my mind not to react.
This gentle voice calling my name.

My eyes fluttered open
 I look at the person who was
talking.
Shock and disbelief crown my
face, I realize it was just a dream.

Strawberry

I think I shall always eat
A fruit as lovely as a berry
A strawberry whose skin looks
as lovely as it taste.

So sweet, so succulent, so
delicious.
My mouth runs water for such
delicacy.
The delicacy of a strawberry.

So soft, so red with such pulpy
radiance.
Oh strawberry, oh juicey
strawberry
Oh sweet fleshy red fruit.

Oh edible berry such sweet liquid
secretion that flow from this juicy
berry, whenever I eat a strawberry
It's so delicious and so nectarous.

Food

Food is something
Sweet to be admired
but never to be trusted.

Food is like an secret.
That burns the tongue
You are waiting hungrily
to past on that sweet story.

Food intoxicating every
bite, every morsel.
So juicy, so finger licking.

Food your fingers itch
just to touch.
You enjoy this company
immensely.

Food your lover, your
best friend.
Never to be part with
This close allies.

Food like sacred Union
Sacred commitment
Secret formula to be
hidden, stored, put aside
and sold to the highest bidder.

Food away to a man's heart.
A peacemaker, a joy maker.
Food a good traveling company.
There's never a celebration
without food.

Food you want
More, more, more
A staff of life.
Food for the soul.

My Vegan Dishes

I love to eat vegan style.
The lushus vegetables are my
favorites dishes.

My vegetable stew
With red peas and carrot, Irish
potato, pumpkin, and cho-cho
cook down in some coconut juice.

How I love my vegan dishes.

My cauliflower cut into small dice
sizes with pap chow
Minced garlic, finely chop onion,
tomatoes, escallion and time.
Flavor to delight with boil yam and
sweet potatoes; delicious.

How I love my vegan dishes.

My boil cassava, and boil banana
with black beans and mushroom,
with coconut juice run down

lace with onion, tomato, garlic and
escallion and time.

I am so delighted to eat my vegan
dishes.

My roast breadfruit with boil Ackee
and broad bean, crush red pepper
and basil for garnish.

Stimulating my taste buds
How I love my vegan dishes.

SERENITY

76. The fountain

77. Wishing on a star

79. Seeking

82. Poetry

84. Tranquility

86. The cloud like the bees

88. Love and hate

89. The Mona Lisa

70. Elizabethan Era

The Fountain

The Fountain is ever tingle
with a drop of elixir.
Springing forth natural source
of joy.

The Fountain naturally a source
of drop, dripping onto the
tongue of life.

A reservoir of liquid energy
Splashing like paint out of
an artist brush on to a
canvas coming to life.

The fountain of pure delight
Intensify pleasuring with just
the right mixture of everlasting
touch.

The fountain a destiny
Of everlasting love.

Wishing on a Star

I close my eyes to make a wish.
I am wishing on a star.
A wish, so perfect.
A wish to be cherish.
As I close my eyes to wish on
a star.

This is the moment.
This very moment.
I pause for a few breathe as I
remember gazing on the stars.
So full and bright, shining into the sky.

I decided I will make a wish,
a wish on a star.
My which so subdue, so soft, so
engendering.

My wish whispering softly in the
ears of the gods, angels and fairies.
Blowing like the wind carrying away
petals of flowers on the wings of the air.

My wish carrying away like flocks of
birds migrating to find comfort in
warm seasons.
My wish, my wish.
As I close my eyes to wish on a star.

Seeking

I am seeking
Seeking away.
Away to go beyond.
Beyond from here.

To somewhere, where
The breezes is pink.
The sky is purple.
And when the sun shines
Stars radiate in a vibrant
rainbow.

I am seeking
Seeking away
Away to go beyond
Beyond from here.

Where my dreams are reality
With every step I take
beautiful flowers grow.
With every breath I takes.
birds sings harmonious melody.

I am seeking
Seeking away
Away to go beyond
Beyond from here.

To the water
Where I swim night and
day and live like a fish.
Where I sings with the mermaid.
Dances with the Dolphins.
And play with adorable sharks.

I am seeking
Seeking away
Away to go beyond
Beyond from here.

Where the world is in peace
and harmony.
And all the bombs, guns, knives.
are thrown away.
And we all live in
Love and togetherness.

I am seeking
Seeking away
Away to go beyond

Beyond from here.

Poetry

Poetry is like fine art
The best a Mona Lisa.

Poetry is like fine wine.
The best a Romanee Conti.

Poetry is like satin,
Sliding off your fingers, so
delicate to be hold.

Poetry music to your ears
Composed in several genres.

Poetry a creation
Sublime of images flowing
from mind to the pencil.
Transforming pages after
pages of beauty.

Poetry many heroic,
many epic, many musical.

Poetry swings with the past

Diverse with the present.
Blowing into the future.

Poetry, literature comprising
poems in verses, languages.
Poetical and sometime
imaginations in any medium.

Tranquility

The tranquility
Of the dirt lay in peace always
on the upside down of trees, houses
animals, and humans carrying on
as usual.

 The tranquility
Of the sky
While the clouds pass all day.
While the sun shines and the
moon and the stars light up the
sky at night.

The tranquility
Of a ship scarcely a ripple from a
far.
With people on deck going and
coming.
Children playing, music by the
patio, laughters.
Lovers on deck gazing beyond
the water.

The tranquility
Of a house, serene yet bold with
music stumping through a window.
Tone of voices as family get together.
And a screeching of a tire from a car
pulling out of the driveway.

Tranquility
The dirt, the sky, a ship scarcely a
ripple from a far.
The house unagitated in the midst
of uproar.

The cloud like the bees

The clouds like the bees
Busy with different duties
To occupy a cloudy mind.

Flowent rivers, springs, fountains,
seas.
What steady lives you live.
While running from a source
of unstoppable supply of water.

Wind that blows so cool on a
hot day.
And windy on a cold day.
How can I forget you.
You speak so softly in my ears
telling me secrets known to
you and only you.

Lovely bushes, trees
You never forget your duties
As you bring forth seeds daily
to replenish this earth.
How sweet and juicy fruits

are.
I taste the nectars of all
your yields.

Life, I feel it within
I look out at many different
life forms.
A fly, a ant, a elephant, man.
We feed off life.
As nature supply us with
everything.

Love and Hate

Love, light shining bright.
Hate, darkness, dull voided.
So separate.
One goes for goodness.
One goes for bad deed.

Love and hate
Can never dwells as one.
Only goodness and mercy.
We will abide by.
All the days of our lives.

Man must always dwells in
light and share love with each
and ever souls creating harmony
amongst mankind.

The Mona Lisa

The Mona Lisa
Stand abreast history.
Leaping through time and space.
Sitting in a museum.
Who was the famous Mona Lisa
Or the Mona Lisa famous only
in a portrait.
Yet she stand proud.
Like a great philosopher.
Yet not much was ever spoken of
the great Mona Lisa.
Is it that she depict a serenity of
a maiden.
The beauty of pure femininity.
The young maiden that sitteth
on a throne.
The throne of simplicity.

Elizabethan Era

The era of unfathomable
depth.
Never before in history.
Has a ruler rule
For such many years.

The queen stand proud.
Proud as a monarch.
As a monument of great service.
To thy country and beyond.

The longest reigning Queen
regnant.
The longest reigning current
monarch.
Oldest, longest serving current
head of state.

A silver jubilee souvenirs.
A golden jubilee souvenirs.
A diamond jubilee souvenirs.
A sapphire jubilee souvenirs.

The first British monarch to
commemorate a sapphire jubilee.
The Queen stand true in all this
By honoring family, state, and
country.
By never renounced her
sovereignty.
Queen Elizabeth 11 sixy-six years
on the throne.

M

THE DEPTH OF LIFE

94. Red

96. I travel

98. Animal or man

100. Time

101. This world

103. Nature is soft

105. Man an autopilot

Red

I see red
As i squeeze my teeth in
the juicery red strawberry.

I see red
As he hand me a beautiful
red rose.

I see red
As I hold the glass of red
pomegranate to my lips.

I see red
As I pass the basket of rosy
red tomatoes.

I see red
As I held the picture with the
red scarlet Ibis up to my face.

I see red
As I look at my dining table
with the bouquet of red tulips,
red orchids and red hibiscus.

I see red
While I was having red chilli
pepper with red beans
delicious.

I see red
As I stand by the patio looking
at the red Bougainvillea flowers.

I see red
As I listen to the sweet whistle
sound of the Northern Cardinal.

I see red
As I think about the hybrid red
sheep lifespan of eighteen years
living only in Iran.

I see red

I Travel

I travel
I was inside the pockets of Gullivers
once as he was washed ashore after
the shipwreck where he played
favorite with the small Lilliputians.

I travel
As I hid behind Jack while he climb
the bean stalk, sneak inside the
castle and steal the giant treasure.

I travel
I was hiding under the Bears
bed while Goldilicks sits in their
chairs, eat some of their porridge
and sleeps in all their beds.

I travel
I was at the Prince ball when
Cinderella drop her glass slippers
at the stroke of twelve while she
flee for safety.

I travel
I was hiding in the closet
shaking with fear as my teeth
chartered and my knees
trembles when little Red Riding
Hood ask the wolf what big teeth
he has as he gobble her up, then
I dashed to called the woodcutter
who chop her out of his belly.

I love traveling
I travel

Animal or Man

Man walk around with all hope
forgotten.
While animal walk around with
poise and pose
Sleek in their upbringing.

Man walk around with a tight
chest, fear gripping at his sleeves.
While animal walk around light
as feathers
No fear, no anger just ease.

Man says problem brews, he
cannot live help, help somebody,
anybody.
Animal lying lazily eaten tummy
full happy, happy they play like
small children.

Man died of many sickness
Whether rich or poor too many
disease.

Animal died not of many sickness
if any.
Just hunt or be hunted.

Man complain of stress and poor
Animal lives, eat, lives

What's the difference between
the proud man and the animal.
Man own's animals yet it seems
animal owns life.

A man may just kick down his
dog because the dog is happier
than him.

Time

Time is nothing but a truck
of sand running out.

Into a bucket.
Grains of sands flowing out.

Onto a table sliding off
Into a hourglass.

To be turn every hour until
the chapter of the day is close.

Shut tight never to be open
but to be remembered.

Like memories trickling out.
Like bees making honey.

Swarming, swarming, swarming.

Until a voice scream no more,
no more, no more.

This World

This world
That we live into never stop
amazing mankind.

This world
Always replenishes itself.
There is no slow just grow.

Days after days.
Months after months.
Years after years.

Every single thing on the
face of this earth is growing.

The trees new budding
every seasons.
The animals new babies every
day.
Humans new babies every day.

But

This world
That we live into never stop
amazing mankind.

This world
Always replenishes itself
There is no slow just grow.

Nature is soft

Nature is soft
Like a baby delicate touch.

Nature is soft
The feeling of the wind
whispering softly in my ears.

Nature is soft
Like the feeling of a lion
fur pressing gentle on your fingers.

Nature is soft
Like snowflakes
flowing gentle to the ground.

Nature is soft
Gentle running your fingers
on a fish soft wet body.

Nature is soft
Like pebbles running through
your fingers.
A hard texture but refine.

Nature is soft
Like honey flowing on
tongue.

Nature is soft
Like beautiful cloud
flowing gentle by in the sky.

Everything about nature is soft
The trees blowing in the wind.
The animal grazing in the meadow.
The cloud, the sea, the mud.

Nature is soft.

Man an autopilot

Man living the life of an autopilot
While he runs behind a scene
that means nothing to him.

We have so many empty
spaces in our lives.
While working the autopilot
shift.
Which we called life.

We crave for something
we cannot at times define
These cravings.

So many of us
Living according to plan
Yet we are heartbroken
and tired of this living.

It's like there is no safe
heaven for living the way
we are living.
There is no peace to flourish

into our hearts.

We so seek what we cannot
define.
Churches at times just don't
mend this craving.

The guide to fulfillment
Man knows not where to find.
So man continues to live the
life of an autopilot.

Still looking.

ABOUT THE AUTHOR

About the Author

Veronia Wilson is the author of
a few poetry collections, her first
young adult novel titled, Searching
For the Mermaid.
All her books are available in print
and ebook format at leading book
retailers.

Discover other titled by Veronia Wilson

Poems:

I am the Emperor: Spiritual Awakening Memoir
Christmas Poems: The Calling of Christmas
Sweet Jamaica Poems
14 Days of Valentine Day

Novel:

Searching For The Mermaid

Made in the USA
Monee, IL
08 July 2026

56552660R00064